NORTHAMPTON

LOOKING BACK

NORTHAMPTON

LOOKING BACK

NORTHAMPTON
Chronicle
& ECHO

at heart  publications

First Published in 2007 by:
Northampton Chronicle & Echo,
Upper Mounts, Northampton, NN1 3HR in
conjunction with
At Heart Ltd, 32 Stamford Street, Altrincham,
Cheshire, WA14 1EY.

Printed and bound by Bell & Bain Ltd., Glasgow

ISBN: 978-1-84547-157-6

NLB001

INTRODUCTION

There was a point, when a team of drivers pulled up at the *Northampton Chronicle & Echo* with several van-loads of boxes filled with dusty old glass plates, when I seriously wondered whether we had done the right thing.

The *Chron* was a modern community newspaper, thriving in the digital age with a flourishing website and the latest image delivery technology... what would we do with all these old boxes?

I need not have worried. Our glass plates project has been a truly great success, thanks to our readers and the hard work and dedication of Peter Clarke, the *Chron's* assistant editor.

From the moment we scanned in the first glass plate, we knew this was going to be a winner. They might be old but the quality of the images was fantastic and we set about creating our Looking Back section.

Almost immediately we were overwhelmed with the response from our readers and handling the Looking Back section and the feedback we received became a lengthy but very rewarding job for Pete.

This book is the result of dozens of those Looking Back pages as well as the responses we have received. Our sincere thanks goes to the hundreds of *Chron* readers who have helped us put it together, and my personal thank-you goes to Pete for all his hard work in collating this publication.

The *Chron* now has a highly successful website and video technology in our photographic department, but as our newspaper enters a new era in the 21st century, we will never forget to cherish the images and stories of the past that have made our town and county great.

Mark Edwards
Editor
Northampton Chronicle & Echo, May 2007

Chron assistant editor Peter Clarke matches glass negatives with readers' responses.

FOREWORD

This book would not have been possible if it were not for readers of the *Chronicle & Echo*, Northamptonshire County Council... and Northamptonshire Fire and Rescue Service! All the pictures in it have been scanned from fragile glass negatives, the fore-runner of photographic film. The negatives were donated to the county council in 1978 when the *Chronicle & Echo* quit its historic Market Square home in Northampton and moved half-a-mile north to new premises at Upper Mounts.

The negatives were used occasionally by historians but had a limited value because very few had any information attached to them. This meant we did not know when they were taken, or why, or who was on the picture.

Then in 1996 the Guildhall Road warehouse where they were being stored caught fire. Incredibly, the negatives were rescued from the heat and even survived damage from the thousands of gallons of water used to put out the massive blaze.

They were taken to Burton Latimer Library where they stayed in a storeroom for nearly 10 years. The cramped conditions were not ideal so the county council asked the *Chron* if we would like them back. "OK," we said, "how many are there?"

"Thirty thousand," was the reply!

By an ironic stroke of luck, the *Chron* had a few years previously switched to digital photography which meant that a former darkroom was lying unused. This was quickly equipped with shelves to hold the glass plates and, after a gap of 27 years, the negatives returned home.

But the old problem remained... we had 30,000 photographs and virtually no information to go with them. We wondered if we published a few in the *Chron* whether our readers would be able to supply the missing information. We need not have worried! Readers loved the new Looking Back feature and very soon letters and emails were flooding in with information.

And so we learned that a sleek Mercedes car pictured at a race meeting was actually driven by Juan Manual Fangio and the meeting was the 1954 British Grand Prix at Silverstone. We were able to name the 1954 Miss Battle of Britain!

Perhaps the most amazing story to have come out of the dusty glass plates so far was the

Chron photographers in the 1950s.

heart-warming tale of a little girl, a doll and a father who was feared to have been killed in the Korean War. We published the picture of father, daughter and doll and very soon had a reply from Gill Cory. She recognised herself aged four in 1953 with the doll her father Ron Clayson had bought her on his release from prisoner-of-war camp. Mr Clayson served with the Northamptonshire Regiment and fought with the "Glorious Glosters" in the famous battle of the Imjin River in 1951. He was captured and survived brainwashing before being released. The full amazing story is told inside Looking Back.

So we would like to dedicate this book to Gill and all the other readers who have put names to faces and been kind enough to write to us with their memories. Without you, this book would not have happened.

Thank you.

Peter Clarke
Assistant Editor
Chronicle & Echo

The *Chron's* appeal for old cine film of Northamptonshire has resulted in a new section on our website. Click on to www.NorthamptonChron.co.uk to see such events as the demolition of Northampton Power Station and the pedestrianisation of Abington Street.

AT
WORK

■ Alan Wigfall was surprised to see a photograph of his late father sitting on top of the old *Chronicle & Echo* building in Northampton Market Square! He writes: "The extension to the building started in April 1952 and the main contractor was Underwood and Weston Ltd of Lady's Lane, Northampton. My father, Joe Wigfall, who was in charge of the contact, is the workman on the right of the photo and died of cancer within three years of this picture being taken."

NLB002

■ This is the blacksmith's in Little Brington, says Richard Harvey, whose grandfather Albert Williams is on the right of the picture. On the left is John Williams.   NLB003

■ David Shrewsbury saw himself in *Looking Back*. He is the taller man in the picture and says: "This photograph was taken in the late 1960s. It records an antique sale at Northampton Auction Galleries in the saleroom at the back of the premises at 37 Sheep Street." The other man is the late Sterry Ashby, the owner of the business. Mr Shrewsbury added: "I joined the firm from school in 1962 and at the time of the photograph I was the manager of the antiques section of the galleries. We held sales about every two months. These were far more interesting sales than the weekly Monday night general chattels auctions held next door, and were held on a Wednesday morning, attracting buyers and dealers from all over the country. A special interest lot must have been on sale for the *Chronicle & Echo* to be present."   NLB004

■ This photograph delighted *Chron* reader Anita Jessop because the man receiving the trophy is her grandfather Leonard Wilson. Mr Wilson, who died 26 years ago, is shown receiving the York Trailer trophy for Lorry Driver of the Year from the manager of the Shell Mex Depot in Northampton, Mr H J Burney. Mr Wilson, who lived in Kingsthorpe, won the prize in a competition in Husbands Bosworth. Mrs Jessop wrote: "As a family we would attend these annual competitions. The tension was immense as he reversed his articulated lorry with such precision up to barriers and you could not get a Rizla paper in between. He would drive in and out of cones and our black good luck cat sat in the cab with him. I always think of him when I am trying to reverse my trailer on the back of my tiny Metro van. He was an amazing grandad, but as they say, behind every successful man is a good woman, so let's not forget Nan who had a very lonely life without him until she died 12 years later. Pap was very competitive, full of life, a great achiever and a great story-teller. My sister and I learned a lot from Pap and subconsciously our characters hold a lot of his traits. Thank you for printing one of his glory moments."

NLB005

■ What we first thought were engine parts were in fact a cable joint box, says ex-East Midlands Electricity Board engineer Tim Cross. He thinks this is two EMEB engineers joining an underground cable and dates the picture to the early 1950s. J Ives and Gervase Forsyth agreed with Mr Cross.

NLB006

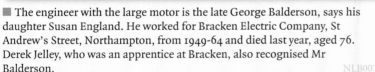 The engineer with the large motor is the late George Balderson, says his daughter Susan England. He worked for Bracken Electric Company, St Andrew's Street, Northampton, from 1949-64 and died last year, aged 76. Derek Jelley, who was an apprentice at Bracken, also recognised Mr Balderson. NLB007

■ Bernard Lawes recognised himself at the age of 22. He writes: "The photo was probably was taken in the winter of 1969-70. The shop is still situated at 233 Wellingborough Road and in those days it was named G S Lawes & Son and sold ironmongery and hardware. Then in 1983 it was re-named Lawes Homecare and still continues to trade as a hardware and cookshop, although I sold the business as a going concern in 2001, to pursue other business interests." NLB008

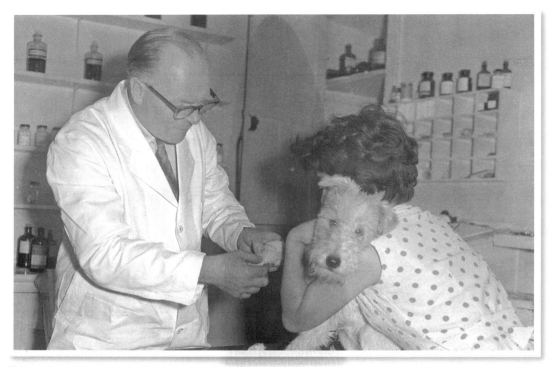

■ Several readers recognised the vet at work. **Phyllis Faulkner wrote:** "He is my dear dad, John 'Jack' Sturgess and was the local PDSA veterinary practitioner for 34 years, from 1941 to 1975. He worked for the PDSA for 48 years and was one of 15 original PDSA Guild members. He was joined by my mum who worked alongside him for 21 years as assistant, secretary and fund-raiser. They were both very dedicated to caring for animals and as a child I can remember feeling so proud when dad was called on by police to recover an injured dog that no-one could get near. It was as if it knew dad was there to help and allowed him to get near enough to treat it. There were so many similar occasions and I know he was very well thought of by the majority of the community. On behalf of my brother and sister, I thank you so much for publishing the photo. It has set off a mass of wonderful memories about two wonderful people. Mr Sturgess's son John thought the picture was taken between the mid-1940s and early 1950s when the dispensary was in Horsemarket. Angie Seelig also recognised Mr Sturgess. She adds: "He broke my heart as a young girl when he had to put my pet guinea pig to sleep." NLB009

■ The man on the right is Alderman J V Collier, Mayor of Northampton in 1954-55, says his son Simon Collier. His father died in All Saints Church on Easter Sunday, 1965, and the doors at the west end of the church were erected in his memory. The projectionist is George Hirons, says his niece Julia Barrett. He worked at Northampton's Ritz Cinema as chief projectionist from 1946 until he retired in 1965. He lived in Kingsthorpe, Northampton, for more than 30 years until his death in 1976. Ken Osborne wrote to tell us all about the projector! He agreed it was at The Ritz in Welford Road, Kingsthorpe, and said it was a Kaylee II with a Peerless arc lamp, RCA stereophonic sound and Varimorph CinemaScope lens. NLB010

■ Former Bassett Lowke employee Ray Stutley remembers the model boat as being the Mercury, a cable-layer built to the scale of 1-96 for ship builders Cammell Laird. Pictured left to right are, Bill Rowe, unknown, unknown, H Sell, C Derry, P Clayton, R Bindon-Blood, H Frost, unknown and R Fuller. Mr Stutley assembled the Mercury in 1962.

NLB011

■ The lone groundsman at the County Ground, Northampton, was Bert Brailsford and the picture was taken in the 1950s, says Christine French, of Duston, Northampton. She used to live in Adnitt Road, just a few doors away from the ground's entrance.

NLB012

■ Michael Rogers recognised himself as the young man toiling in a Northampton workshop. "I think I was about 16 at the time," he recalled. "I used to work in a little workshop at W H Johnson in Abington Street, opposite Notre Dame Girls School. I used to work sharpening things like shears and stuff like that." NLB013

■ This is the Esso depot at Heathfield Way, Kings Heath, Northampton, around 1950, says William Judge. He recognises depot manager Reg Ellis who became a church warden at All Saints.

NLB014

■ Mary Mass and June Tew (née Coleman) recognised themselves in the new closing room of Manfield's shoe factory, Wellingborough Road, Northampton, in the 1950s.

NLB015

■ The man with a figure of Christ on the cross was Frank Flavell, says his granddaughter Julia Bellham. "He was foreman in charge of the building of the Roman Catholic church in Park Avenue North. My dad, Frank Jnr, also worked on the site. The year may have been 1953 or 54." Brian Harding also spotted St Gregory's Church and says the cross is still there today. The parish priest at the time was Fr Eric Phillips, he added. NLB016

■ This is the opening dairy show sale at the new Northampton Attested Market in the early 1950s, says John Mather, who is the auctioneer pictured. The cow is a dairy shorthorn.

NLB017

■ Mrs B Bromwich tells us her husband David recognised himself in the picture with fellow students at Kettering Road Secondary School. He is on the right, bending down. The name of the teacher was Mr King, he believes. Mr Bromwich went on to Northampton School of Art, then did his National Service before teaching art at Cherry Orchard School and Lings Upper School, Northampton.

NLB018

■ We ran a sequence of cold store pictures which rang bells for Roy Mallard who worked in an adjacent company in Abington Square, Northampton. The man with the bowler is Major Lucas, the owner. NLB019

■ "This picture brought back good childhood memories," wrote Bob Murray. "It was the demolition of the old St John's Street railway station, an old play haunt of mine, living in Victoria Prom for all my youth, 1949-70. We used to climb onto the flat roof of the entrance in St John's Street to get in and light bonfires and smoke Nelson Tipped cigarettes and run and jump down the old bridge parapets on the corner of Victoria Prom and Swan Street to make our escape from the local bobby." Mike Thompson said the picture was taken when it was being demolished in the 1960s. T N Parker said the station closed in 1939 and just one man was reputedly responsible for its demolition! Chris Osborne tells us he has a set of drawings of the station and one day will build a model of it for historical record.

NLB020

■ This is Robert Wright, pictured at Boughton, says his granddaughter Patricia Brittle. Robert lived at 6 Boughton and died in 1957.

NLB021

■ This is Wappenham blacksmith Reg Abbott, says his grandson David Abbott.

NLB022

DRAMA

■ These two amateur dramatic productions have been identified by Alison
Dunmore. The picture on the right was taken at the now-demolished Masque Theatre in Thenford
Street, Northampton, on March 20, 1970, this shows four of the cast of Noel Coward's *Hay Fever*. From left they
are: Dennis Phillips, Diana Hill, Beryl Andrews and David White. The second picture shows Northampton Theatre Guild's very first production, in 1953, *Thunder Rock*. From left are Arthur Cockell, Leslie Necus and Don Anderson. Both plays were directed by Alison's late husband, Maurice, who was for many years the *Chron's* music
critic. Renee Necus also recognised her husband in *Thunder Rock*.
NLB023 & NLB024

■ Memories came flooding back for Masque Theatre members after this picture was published. Jean McNamara wrote: "This is Bryan Hall and me in a scene from *Everything in the Garden*, a black comedy presented in the Masque's tiny theatre in Thenford Street. Bryan and I are still actively involved in amateur theatre and in July, 2005 I directed *A Month of Sundays* at the new Moulton Theatre in which Bryan played the leading part, a mere 42 years after the picture in the C&E."   NLB025

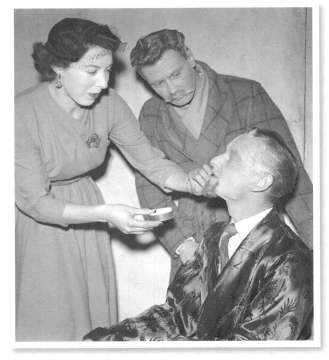

■ Jean McNamara again recognised herself on one of these old pictures! This time the Masque Theatre's production was *Venus Observed* by Christopher Fry in December 1953. She is attaching a beard to William Ford at the dress rehearsal. The other actor is William Brightman, who turned professional and was described in *The Stage's* obituary, after his early death, as one of the unsung, hardworking stalwarts of north country rep.   NLB026

■ Two readers recalled this school nativity play, memorable for featuring a pig's head on a platter! Jacqueline Winter (née Lyon) said the play was put on by the junior school in Main Road, Far Cotton, Northampton, around 1953-54. It was called *The Boar's Head* and Mrs Winter played the part of Mary. Mr Adams was the headmaster, this was Mr Elliot's class and the two girls dressed the same in the back are the Lawrence twins. Our former *Chron* colleague Rod Burdett was also on the picture, in the second row from the back, just above the first shepherd. NLB027

■ The celebrity signing autographs is actor Arnold Peters, pictured with his wife Beryl, writes their daughter Caroline Windsor. It was taken at Wilton, near Daventry, in 1953 when Mr Peters was playing Len Thomas in the radio series *The Archers*. He is still in the long-running soap, now playing Brummie businessman Jack Woolley. NLB028

■ Several readers recognised children's entertainer Mr Pastry (Richard Hearne), who was a well-known TV star and died in 1979. NLB029

■ This was taken at Daventry Grammar School in 1953 or 54, says Marge Nightingale. Her brother David Billingham remembered the play was *The Rivals* and produced by English teacher Jock Campbell. In the cast were Malcolm Coleman, Roger Stephenson, Margaret Hodgkinson, Freddie Shoesmith, Janet Holden, John Ashby, Joe Williams and Martin Hardiman. NLB030

■ The venue is St Alban's Church Hall, Northampton, says Vera Witts, and the dancers in the first picture include Mrs Gilbert Wood, Eleanor Howland and Norah Midwinter. The two in the second picture are Margaret Furniss and Charles Bailey. Mr Bailey is an amazingly spritely 94-year-old, residing at St John's Home, Wellingborough Road, she added. She also spotted in the audience her mother-in-law Mrs Dorothy Witts. Eleanor Howland recognised herself, Milly Cook, Mabel Latchford and Evelyn Wood and confirmed the other names.

NLB031 & NLB032

■ Cliff Billing recognised himself and Mary Greaves (née Haddon) in Northampton Amateur Operatic Company's production of *South Pacific* at the ABC Cinema (now The Jesus Centre) in 1964. Cliff is now in his 58th year singing with the company, of which he is president. NLB033

■ The lady on stage is Virginia, Marchioness of Northampton. She has the robe she wore when she attended the Coronation in 1953. She gave talks on this to the Women's Institute at Castle Ashby, says Joan Burge. NLB034

■ The sign mentioning the Palace of Varieties is not a plaque but an enamel advertising sign, says Tony Perrett. He adds: "They were blue with white lettering. I have one, there is one in Abington Park Museum and I know of at least one other. The Palace of Varieties was on the corner at the junction of Gold Street and Horseshoe Street." According to the website www.northampton.org.uk, the Palace of Varieties opened in 1901. Sue Edwards also has one of the signs which she bought from an antiques shop in Kettering Road. Lisa Cottrell added: "The shop in the photograph belonged to my grandfather, William Christopher Cross. It was in Wellingborough Road, quite close to Abington Square. He was a bespoke shoemaker. The picture must have been taken between 1946-60. My mother has no idea why the 'Palace of Varieties' sign above the shop was there. It is interesting for us, particularly as I have worked in the theatre profession for 30 years. Maybe it was a 'sign'!"

NLB035

■ Winifred Bradbury was delighted to see a picture of her late father William Aistrope looking at a bust of Shakespeare in the foyer of the Royal Theatre in the 1950s. She writes: "My dad attended a Shakespeare play as a guest of the *Chronicle & Echo* because he had written a couple of scathing letters to you about the amount of time devoted to Shakespeare on the television. I still have the cuttings from the dear old *Chron*."

NLB036

■ Rosalind Gibson wrote: "Yes, it's me being made-up by Miss Margaret Gillingham. It was 1955 and the play was Charles Kingsley's *Water Babies*, being performed by our class of Weston Favell C of E School in the Schools' Drama Festival held at Moulton Secondary Modern School. Others in the picture are Barbara Maycock, Susan Pinches, Linda Dyer and Richard Seaby (I think!). It was certainly some of the happiest days of my life, under the headship of Mr Harry Hawkins, his wife Gladys and Mr Robert Crook. The Looking Back feature is one of the best in the *Chron*." NLB037

■ These are fifth form pupils of Northampton High School performing *The Princess And The Swineherd* at the Guildhall, says Hilda Hadley, née Williams. She writes: "The princess in the chair was Anita Mobbs and should have been crying but she had her head bowed because she couldn't stop laughing. This made it very difficult for the servants in pointed hats not to giggle. I was the servant bending over the princess." NLB038

BACK FROM KOREA

MEMORIES OF A happy homecoming for a Korean War veteran were sparked by one of our *Looking Back* photographs.

We published a photograph from our glass negative collection of a man and a little girl in the old Clipper Café in Northampton, which had been taken in 1953.

Gill Cory contacted us to say that the picture showed her at the age of four with her late father, Ron Clayson. It had been taken immediately after he returned from a two-year internment in a Chinese prisoner-of-war camp.

Mr Clayson, of Westone, who died from cancer in December 2003, aged 82, was a member of the 2nd Battalion Northamptonshire Regiment and fought with the "Glorious Glosters" at the battle of the Imjin River in Korea.

This has gone down in history as a gallant English victory, as the action enabled the advance of the Chinese army to be halted. Many men were captured during the action, in April 1951, but the battle meant that the United Nations forces were able to regroup and the Chinese spring offensive was defeated.

Mr Clayson was one of the men taken prisoner, but for his family waiting at home in England his fate was uncertain.

Mrs Cory said it was only through the *Chronicle & Echo* that they had first realised her father was still alive after being captured.

"He was 'missing in action' after the battle; however, my mum recognised my dad in a photograph in the *Picture Post*, showing prisoners of war bathing in a river in North Korea," she said.

"She contacted the *Chronicle & Echo*, who were able to confirm that it was indeed my Dad."

Mr Clayson was held prisoner from 1951 until 1953. While in the camp, he suffered severe dysentery and was forced to watch communist propaganda films by Chinese soldiers who tried to brainwash him.

Fortunately he discovered an ability to "switch off" during these lectures, as those who did not attend were refused medical treatment.

He was released in June 1953 and travelled back to England by boat, where his daughter Gill was waiting to greet him.

"I was four years old when he returned to the UK, and when we met him off the boat he promised to buy me the biggest, best doll ever, which I called Mary," Mrs Cory recalled.

"The photograph was taken on the day we went to buy the doll.

"My Dad was a modest man, who had been through a great deal and shied away from publicity, but he finally agreed to let the *Chronicle & Echo*

NLB039

photographer take a photograph of us in the Clipper."

After surviving the horrors of the war and imprisonment, Mr Clayson returned to work at British Rail's signal department, where he stayed for the next 40 years. But the memories of the bloody battle he had been involved in remained with him until he died.

After his death, his widow, Joan, told the *Chron*: "He used to say he could still hear the Chinese coming over the hill screaming and blowing their whistles.

"He told me he expected to die then. He was amazed when they just took him prisoner.

"He was such a strong man. He used to say he was not in pain, but you could see in his face that he was."

Mr Clayson's coffin was covered with his regimental flag and the medals he won distinguishing himself in battle.

IN UNIFORM

■ Two readers supplied information on this picture of the Royal Pioneer Corps at their training headquarters, Simpson Barracks, Wootton, in 1964. Bob Harmston said the two men in white coats both worked at Adams Bakery. The one on the right is Fred James, who used to live first in Queen Eleanor Road, Far Cotton, and then in Witham Way, Kings Heath. Fred and he first met in the army in Germany in 1946 and became firm friends. Mr N Moreton from Thornhill said he believed the occasion was the marking of the 50th anniversary of the Pioneer Corps, which was formed from the old Labour Corps in 1914.

NLB040

■ The Northamptonshire Regiment Association told us that this was taken at Loughborough College Airfield on May 14, 1954, and shows Princess Alice, the regiment's Colonel-in-Chief, inspecting the troops. Behind her is commanding officer N J Dixon.

NLB041

■ The princess is shown talking to Band Sgt Major Cyril Holland with RSM "Dickie" Bird looking on.

NLB042

■ John Nightingale reckons this is the control room at The Mounts Fire Station, Northampton, and the date is 1952-54. A crew from the BBC are interviewing Brian Lawrence from St Mary's Church Lads' Brigade. The lads came second in a competition for private fire brigades and were given a short training course at the fire station. The BBC programme was run adjacent to Dick Barton Special Agent. Brian Lawrence became manager of the Grosvenor Centre, Northampton, and retired a few years ago. NLB044

■ The ladies building the outdoor oven in the 1950s were a Civil Defence group, writes Mrs Eva Edwards, who is in the centre of the picture. She adds: "One Sunday we cooked for about 60 Territorial Army soldiers who were on manoeuvres outside the town. It was getting near the time when the meal should have been ready and it wasn't. We all set to and sliced the meat and fried it. Everyone helped and the meal was shipped out on time."

NLB045

■ Mr D E Gibbs recognised his mother, Northampton Mayor Maud Gibbs. Former police cadet Dan Reid said it was the annual inspection of Northampton Borough Police and he was there! Ex-Sgt H Dickens wrote to say the year was 1964 or 65 and also pictured are Chief Constable Mr D R Baker and HM Inspector of Constabulary Commander W J A Willis. The diver, agreed Mr Reid and Mr Dickens, was Sgt Michael Stevenson, who was in charge of the underwater search unit. Former councillor Trevor Bailey and B Watts also recognised Mayor "Maudy" Gibbs, who represented Delapre Ward for Labour.

NLB046

■ John Burt says the stern-looking nurse is Sister Dora Derham, who was in charge of Connolly Lodge at St Crispin Hospital, Northampton. This was confirmed by D V Lloyd, who says: "My aunt Miss Dora Derham was senior sister of St Crispin Hospital until her retirement in 1961 after 55 years service at the same hospital. She started at the age of 15 in the kitchens and progressed onto nursing the wounded soldiers during the 1914-18 war, eventually becoming senior sister in charge of the convalescent ward. In 1955 she was awarded the BEM in the birthday honours list for services to nursing." NLB047

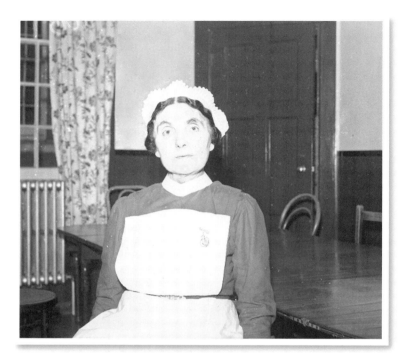

■ John Curtis says this is the now-demolished Quebec Barracks at Wootton around 1954-55 and the officer on the right is Major (later Lt Col) E M Goodale. In the centre is Captain (later Major) Donald Baxter. NLB048

■ Ex- Private K V Perryman, who still remembers his National Service Army number, says this was a passing out parade at Quebec Barracks around 1953-54. He recognised Major Goodale, commanding officer at the depot.

NLB049

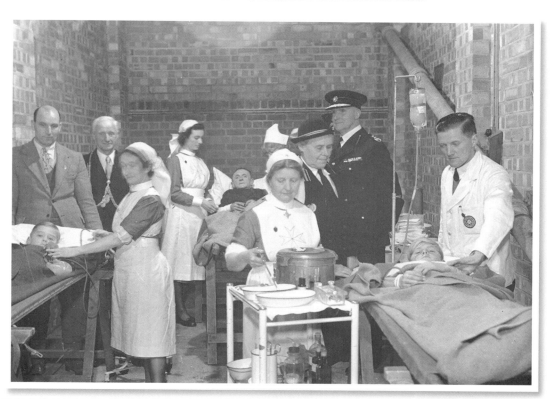

■ Majorie Fryer recognised her late mother Amy Fryer as the St John nurse in the centre of the picture. Behind her is Mrs Edith Carpenter.

NLB050

■ The daughter and wife of this soldier both emailed the *Chron* to tell us he is Gordon Sparkes. Mrs Mary Sparkes said he was stationed in Berlin for almost three years and served in the Intelligence Corps. The picture was taken in October 1953. His daughter Kathryn Ross added that she was born in Berlin. NLB051

■ Margaret Burditt (née Harrison) recognised herself on this picture at celebrations to mark the golden jubilee of the Girls' Life Brigade, now Girls' Brigade. She is the one in uniform and she was able to name Joy Spencer, Joan Stibbards and Sylvia Martin. NLB052

■ Esme Godden and Sheila Woodhams both identified Charlotte Nelson, matron of Northampton General Hospital from 1938-54 receiving a bouquet, probably on her retirement. Standing next to her is Madeleine Punch, matron of Daventry Hospital, who adds former nurse Sheila, was very interested to see the picture in the *Chron.*
NLB053

■ Some of the St John Nursing Cadets were recognised by Janet Barton as her sister Pat Rain, Diana Julian and Margaret Draper. They met at the Gaumont Cinema restaurant, Northampton, every week.
NLB054

■ We guessed correctly when we thought these were Northampton Air Cadets. Mr C Osborne writes: "The officer half visible is Flight Lieutenant Ken Pearson, commanding officer of 5F (Northampton) Squadron of the Air Training Corps. At a later date he served as Mayor of Northampton. The cadet in the front row extreme right is myself and the location is the squadron's old headquarters in Bausholme Meadow. The date would be between 1952-56." NLB055

■ Retired *Chron* journalist Bob Shaw recognised most of the people in this picture. He says it was a two-man first aid competition in the late 1960s. The judge with the board on the left is Dr Sharpe, the St John County Surgeon at the time. The St John team was from the Kingsthorpe Division and attending the patient is the late Gordon Ross and leaning over him is Alan Boaden, who more recently was the St John County Commissioner for Northamptonshire until he handed over the reins. Roger Darby also recognised Dr John Sharpe who he said lived and practised from a house in Abington Avenue. He was Roger's family doctor and a great character.

NLB056

The *Chron* was delighted to correct a 50-year-old injustice and show a picture of Northampton St John Ambulance Cadet Brian Blunt. Brian was not visible on the original photograph of cadets receiving a trophy but sent us this picture of himself, when he was part of the trophy-winning first aid team. NLB057

SCENES

■ This was probably taken during the 1953 Coronation celebrations in The Headlands, between Wellingborough Road and Birchfield Road, Northampton, says Bryon Dunn who grew up in The Headlands.

NLB058

■ Many readers had fond recollections of visits to Abington Library, Northampton. Maeve Orr, who is the library supervisor, writes: "The church became a library in 1939, so I think this photo must date back to the 1940s. It is a beautiful picture and really captures the atmosphere and character of this lovely building, which is a thriving library in the heart of the community in Abington. Today it looks very similar but of course the beautiful long wooden table has been replaced by the computers!" Raymond Coles, of Sywell, told us: "I used to go there as a child with an evacuee we had at the time. I used to go about three times a week." Mrs Hawkins, of Pattishall tells us the area beyond the arch used to be the children's section. And Margaret Beswick, of Lings, writes: "Anyone unfamiliar with the area might think it a place of worship and be surprised at its actual purpose. Having been brought up in Abington it is well known to me." Thanks also to Vanessa Claypole, Ellen Hackett, Sharon Green, Hilda Carr, Lisa Hayward, Tony Ward and Bob Shaw who all contacted us to identify the picture.

NLB059

■ More than a dozen readers emailed having recognised this picture as Marefair, Northampton, viewed from Black Lion Hill. You pointed out the trees in front of St Peter's Church, George Orme men's outfitters, Gordon's Commercial Hotel, much favoured by travelling salesmen, the Black Lion pub, The Athenian restaurant, the Taj Mahal restaurant, Kings butchers and Walter Miles car breakers. One reader even named the car as a Morris Series E!

NLB060

■ Information on this series of pictures was sent in by Jennifer Fuller, on behalf of Margaret and Charlie Dilks. The were all taken in Dodford, near Daventry, and show Mr Dilks collecting water from a spring, Nora Edginton using the pump on The Green and Dorothy Goode and her dog fetching water from the village stream. In the background is the house now known as Quietways, where the Dilkses lived. Mr Dilks thinks the pictures were taken in 1954 before Dodford was served with a metalled road and before the stream was narrowed to its present size.

NLB061, NLB62 & NLB63

■ The row of shops in Wellingborough Road, Northampton, was recognised by Ruth Burgess. Her father worked for Kingstone, whose head office was in Leicester. Her mother, who is 99, remembered all the stores and shopped in some of them!

NLB064

■ The Cenotaph near All Saints Church, Northampton, in the 1950s with The Black Boy Hotel and County Hall behind it. The roof of the Guildhall can be seen on the skyline.

NLB065

■ The mystery of the road covered in mud was cleared up by Mrs B Elworthy who says it was Peverels Way, St James, Northampton, in 1952-53. Only two-thirds of the road was made up at that time but was finished in 1952.

NLB066

■ The dovecote at Denton is still standing, says Edwin Cawley, but is now surrounded by houses. Mr Cawley adds: "I have five tapes I have made of stories handed down to me by my father and grandparents, some of them about the Dovecote. They used to feed the pigeons and the owner used to catch them by closing the trap door at the base of the cupola."

NLB067

■ When the well at Brackley ran dry in 1953, the Royal Army
Ordnance Corps, which had its base at nearby Turweston, was asked
to help, says David McCombie, of Brackley. It supplied personnel and
bowsers and he was one of the soldiers detailed to carry out this duty.

NLB068

■ Lots of readers wrote in with explanations for the queue of people.
All agreed they were waiting to get into the cinema in Abington
Square, Northampton... but there were several different ideas as to
what was showing. A D Hiam thought it was the Morecombe and Wise
Show in 1980 or 81, Paul Dunn thought it was for Rolling Stones
tickets and John Canning thought it may have been for the Beatles.
Mrs A Finch admitted that she did not know the reason for the queue
but said she used to be the manageress of the wallpaper and paint
shop the people are waiting by.

NLB069

■ This is Daventry town centre. The Moot Hall is in the centre and the phone box, which we at first thought was painted white, was actually made of concrete. The Moot Hall is now an Indian restaurant. Thanks to Jean Warwick, Guy Gibbins, David Blackburn, Mr C Arnull, Brian Coward, Jo Walton and *Chron* columnist David Saint for supplying information.   NLB070

■ Great Houghton Hall after a fire in the roof in 1954. Gillian Barnes told us the hall had been purchased by Mr O E Barnes from the Finnemore family. In September 1955 Great Houghton Preparatory School was founded in the building.

NLB071

The picture of the family occupying the wooden huts could have been taken in the late 1940s at the Royal Oak Army barracks in Braunston Road, Daventry, says Mrs R M Wills. The camp was used by homeless ex-service men and their families. Eventually Daventry council adopted the site and provided the squatters with basic amenities.

NLB072

There was quite a debate in the *Chron* as to whether this was was Kingsthorpe Mill or Coleman's Mill. The argument was settled by David Coleman, grandson of the original owners of Coleman's Mill. He sent us a picture of his family's mill which was between Kingsthorpe and Harlestone Firs, and where his father was born in 1896. The two mills are of similar appearance but this is definitely Kingsthorpe Mill. NLB073

■ Church Street, Boughton was identified by Peter Storey, Lucy Bell and Peggy York, who added that she was born in a cottage just off the picture. The pub is the Whyte Melville. NLB074

■ Ken Nicholl identified these buildings at Greens Norton. He writes: "The buildings are still there today and were originally built for the Land Army at the start of World War Two. The buildings were then used as a prisoner-of-war camp. After the war the buildings were used as a Youth Hostel and the YHA sign is still visible on the water tower. Part of the Youth Hostel was removed when a local building contractor bought the site in 1984, developed half of it for his own offices/stores, and sold the remainder to Greens Norton Playing Field Association. The contractor left in 1994 and eventually the site was sold to Greens Norton Parish Council which developed it as phase one of a new community centre." Reader C S Berry's mother was warden of the youth hostel from 1960-75. NLB075

■ Jean Dowdy (née Eckford) quite rightly took us to task for describing her father's newspaper kiosk near All Saints Church as a "shack". She writes: "It was well constructed and was allowed to stand there by the council in 1919 after my father was wounded and lost one of his legs in World War One. With the support of the British Legion and the helpfulness of the council, he was allowed to site his kiosk in the town centre. He was then able to earn a living for his wife and three children and sold many thousands of *Chronicles* and *Echos*." Mr Eckford died in 1924 but the kiosk remained until the 1960s or 70s, she adds. NLB076

■ Ray Whiting told us this is Abington Park lake with its three islands.

NLB077

■ Janet Roff and Richard Coleman both agree this old railway carriage was on the allotments off Towcester Road, Far Cotton, Northampton. Mr Coleman said it was still there in 2004.

NLB078

RAIL TRAGEDY

FIFTEEN PEOPLE died on September 21, 1951, when a Princess class locomotive bound from London to Liverpool left the rails and plunged down an embankment at Weedon, followed by eight coaches. *Chron* reporter Philip Cockbill was the first journalist on the scene and found the engine's fireman, miraculously uninjured.

The fireman said that the train had just emerged from the Stowe Hill tunnel when the front of the locomotive started jumping around and then the engine rolled over and went down the embankment.

His driver was dug out of a pile of coal and was also uninjured, although he was sent to Northampton General Hospital for observation.

The scene of the crash was just two miles from another rail disaster in August 1915 when the Irish Mail crashed outside the tunnel. Nine died on that day.

NLB081

NLB082

SPORT

■ The hockey players were a touring team of the Midlands called the Bacchanalians, who were good drinkers, recalls George Short, former captain of Northampton and County hockey side and an England umpire. The picture was taken on the Northampton Brewery Company ground behind the Spinney Hill Hotel. Mr Short played with or against five of the men pictured but can only name the goalkeeper, Sammy McMillan, a Northampton player.

NLB083

■ The cyclists were at the start of one of the legs of the Milk Race and the photos were taken in front of The Racecourse Pavilion in May or June 1968, says Nick Kelk, who adds: "I took the morning off school to collect their autographs." Richard Mackaness confirms this and remembers: "The attending support cars had the registration letters 'MOO' and the race was sponsored by the Milk Marketing Board." NLB084

NLB085

■ Sharleyne Barber says: "This picture was the prize-giving of the Phipps darts league presented at the Salon. The ladies in the photo were the winners of the A section, they played for the King's Arms." Eileen Stewart adds: "What a pleasant surprise to see the picture of my old dart team from the King's Arms. I played for them for 15 years and we won the winter and summer league for 11 years running. Back row from left: Flo Bustin, Me, Georgina Levy, Eileen Miller, Doll Tapp, Doreen Baker and front from left, Floss Robinson, Bette Law, Glad Blades (captain), Joyce Benton, Rona Kirkton. Sadly only five of us are left now."

NLB086

■ The *Chron* editor commented that looking through our dusty archive of 30,000 glass photographic negatives was like panning for gold. Well, we certainly found some nuggets this time... King George VI and Queen Elizabeth no less! The pictures were taken between the wars, probably at the Pytchley Hunt, when the royal couple could have been just the Duke and Duchess of York. Despite an appeal in the *Chron* we never did manage to find out who the king's side-saddle-mounted companion was.

NLB087

NLB088

■ The showjumper is Joan Sutton, says her sister, Margaret Alcock, of Scaldwell, and the picture was taken at Manor Farm, Hanging Houghton, in 1953, when Joan was 17. She had won a competition at Harringay and the *Chron* photographed her riding Fair Lady.   NLB089

■ George Rowland, of Hartwell, says this is him receiving a swimming shield at The Mounts Baths, Northampton. Donald Loe, late of the 2nd Northampton St Giles Cubs, recognised the lady as Miss Furniss, the Cubs' District Commissioner for Northampton.

NLB090

■ The ladies playing bowls were snapped in 1961 at Kettering Lodge Bowls Club. On the left is Ethel Willson and her partner is Jessie Freeman. They who won the NWCBA pairs competition and then the EWBA national pairs. They played for Kettering Ladies BC, adds Jan Hunt.

NLB091

■ These pictures from the 1955 British Timken Show in Northampton brought back memories for two readers. The pickaxe-swinger was William Culverhouse, writes his granddaughter Gillian Knight. He was born in 1883 and died in 1966. He ran Northampton Amateur Athletics Club for most of his life and appeared regularly at local shows. The pick-axe swinging was his party piece. He would have represented Britain at the Olympic Games if they had not been cancelled because of World War One. He played rugby for the Saints and his pride and joy was his England cap. Ann Jones added that the man nearest the camera performing a shoulder stand was Stan Cooper.

NLB092 & NLB093

■ Pat Skipworth recognised her late father Bert Basford front right in this darts group. The shorter man standing behind him is his brother Bill. She adds: "I still have the darts that my father used. He made them himself and gave them to me when I started playing in the early 1970s. Thank you for printing this picture. It has brought back some wonderful childhood memories."

NLB094

■ This is the opening meet of the Grafton Foxhounds on the village green at Blakesley in the early to mid-1950s, says Doug Blake. The trees were felled in 1976 after suffering Dutch elm disease, he adds.　　NLB095

■ Several readers recognised the newly-formed Northampton Amateur Boxing Club, pictured in 1953. John Morris, then a junior reporter on the *Chron*, was founder-secretary and specialised in sport, eventually becoming the first sports editor of BBC Radio Northampton. He was general secretary of the British Boxing Board of Control from 1986-2000. John is now president of the Northampton club. He also recognised the trainer, the late Harry Reynolds and his son Roy, now a member of the committee. Brian Cayton is also on the committee. Stephen Megeary adds that the picture was taken at The Trades Club in Overstone Road, now the Double Top Club. Peter Cripps is also on the picture and adds some more names: Keith Lamb, Tony Mann, Mike Ruddy and Mr Mann.　　NLB096

■ Mr Morris says this picture was taken around 1954 and in the group are club coach Harry Reynolds, Brian Cayton, Derek Snow, Tony Mann, Fred Cayton and Dick Kitchener. Tony Mann's grandson Malcolm has this year been registered by the club, making a four-generation connection with his family. NLB097

■ The boxer posing is Keith Lamb, at that time a Midland Area welterweight champion of British Railways and the Leicestershire, Rutland and Northants champion as well, added Mr Morris.
NLB098

■ Cobblers player Laurie Brown, who went on to play for Arsenal, Spurs and Norwich, is pictured during the 1959-60 season, says Colin Eldred.　NLB099

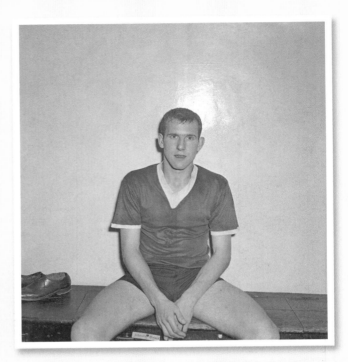

■ "Considering the spectacular transformation that has taken place over recent years, I am not surprised you didn't recognise this much-televised rugby pitch," writes Gordon Currey after we first published this picture. "It is of course the now magnificent Franklin's Gardens, looking towards the lake end. The two players whose faces you can clearly see are, on the right, Andy Johnson and in the middle of the maul Clive Daniels. In the background is the old scoreboard which was usually manned by some of the local school kids who would get jeers from us common folk on the Gordon Terrace if they put the wrong score up." A D Hiam also recognised the venue.　NLB100

■ This brought back memories of Northampton Archery Club for Michael Bull who says the man second left is Bill Day who had a fish and chip shop in Abington Square. The other man was Paddy Flynn who once had the rare distinction of scoring six golds with six arrows, which Michael says is like scoring a hat-trick in the Cup Final! Keith and Cynthia Tunnicliff say this was a mixed archery match in the late 1950s or early 1960s at the British Timken sports ground, Duston. The lady drawing arrows from the target is Phyllis Thompson and they agreed the man with the cap is Paddy Flynn, who was the county archery coach. NLB101

■ Barry and Martin Buckby also recognised the British Timken sports fields but were more interested in this equestrian picture. It features their father Raymond (dark jacket, tie and glasses), who died in October 2004. The child on the horse to his right is probably Martin and the boy directly behind him Barry. The boy holding the reins is thought to be a third brother, David. NLB102

■ Tony Botterill and David Cox both recognised Northampton schools football team of 1953-54. Mr Botterill is in the centre of the front row with hands clasped. Others were Bernard Hart, David Cox, Alan Broadbent, David Sibley, John Darlow, Geoff Warnes, J Cowan and Barry Bushell. Mr Cox, who is fourth from the left, front row, also recognised Ronald Shiperley, John Collins and David Wright. He says they beat South Shields 3-1.

NLB103

■ This is the Northampton Malt Shovel pub bowls team in around 1952, says Ken Malin and Mrs M Hilton, whose late fathers were in the team. Mr Malin thinks the trophy may have been the Crockett Cup.

NLB104

TRANSPORT

■ Ken Brown is the scooterist pictured with a trendy Guy Fawkes in the early 1960s. He says it was a Bonfire Night party and social gathering near Hardwick of the town's two main scooter clubs, the Vespa Club of Northampton and Northants Lambretta and Scooter Club.

NLB105

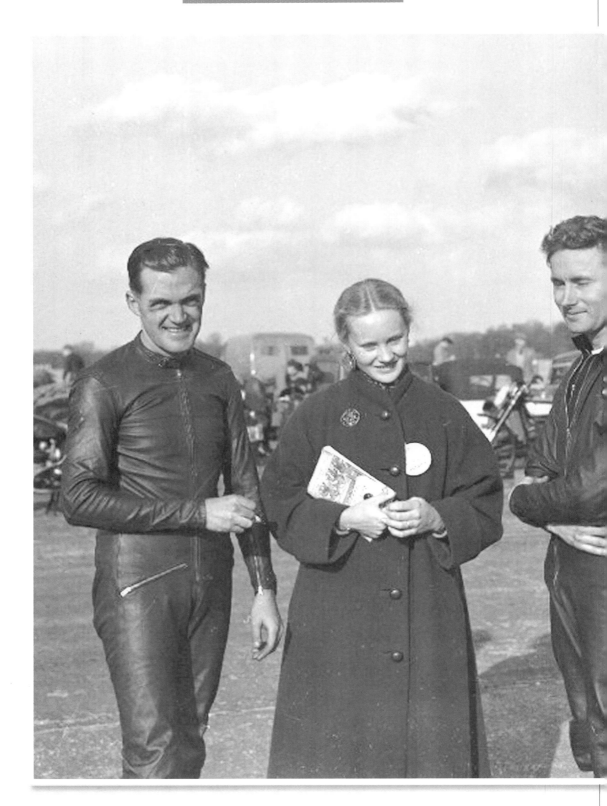

■ "All these men are in the history books as 'great legends' ", veteran
Northampton motorcycle racer Mick Hemmings, himself a bit of a legend, told
the *Chron*. They were snapped at a meeting at Silverstone in the 1950s and in
picture one is Ray Amm, number one works Norton rider, his wife Jill, and on
the right, Derek Farrant, AJS works rider.   NLB106

Picture two, says Mick, shows "the invincible Geoff Duke" with the Gilera he
rode for the works team. Veteran motorcyclist Ted Cotton added that Bernard
Burbidge is standing second from left in picture two.   NLB107

NLB108

■ We really struck gold with these pictures! This is the 1954 British Grand Prix at Silverstone and Roger Watson was there on the Friday practice as an 11-year-old. The man with the folded arms standing in front of the Maserati is Italian driver Alberto Ascari, who died later that year at Monza.
The Mercedes has a streamlined body which proved unsuccessful and only completed at Silverstone in 1954 and at the French Grand Prix. It was driven by the legendary Juan Manuel Fangio, says Roger.

NLB109

■ Bus expert John Child has provided several captions for us. This, he says, is Fish Street, Northampton around 1954 judging from the livery of the double-decker.

NLB110

■ Northampton Corporation Bus VV 8932 is in the background. This bus was in service from April, 1945, until September 1957, says John Child. It was part of a batch of 22 similar vehicles in use at that time, one of which, VV 8934, is currently being restored at a museum in Lincoln having been in a scrapyard for 30 years before being rescued from the cutters torch in 1990. "Photographs of the rear of vehicles are in fact quite rare," said Mr Child. "Most people photograph them from the front. However, for model makers and bus restorers, rear photographs are very helpful." Mr Child thought the picture was taken in 1953 or 54 to publicise the introduction of lollipop men and women.   NLB111

■ This is Lawrence Cummings, a bus enthusiast and the accompanying article was in the *Northampton Independent*, in the autumn of 1953, Patrick Rawlinson told the *Chron*. The heading was "A strange bus and he is thrilled". NLB112

■ Brian Burbidge, owner of B O Burbidge, of Northampton Road, Blisworth, is on the extreme left of this group, says Gordon Davidson. He did not know who the other two were but the scooter was a Phoenix, made between 1957 and 64. NLB113

■ The petrol pump attendant during this fuel rationing spell in the 1950s was Robert Slinn, who used to live in Fife Street, St James, Northampton, says his son-in-law W K J Earl. The driver does not look too happy at being offered only three gallons at Mulliners in Northampton town centre. NLB114

■ The rally crew is brother and sister John and Joan Sunley, who were preparing for the 1954 *Daily Express* National Motor Rally in their blue Sunbeam Talbot car. Joan, now Mrs Tice, recalls they finished the rally in good style but can't remember if they were placed. Her brother was just 18 at the time and she was 21. NLB115

■ The bike repairer was Bob Shakeshaft, whose bicycle shop was in Wellingborough Road, Northampton, says his daughter Joan Ward. He opened the shop shortly after World War Two and retired at the age of 70 in about 1975. He was closely associated with the Invicta cycling club and built many racing bikes for members. John Meacock also remembered the shop.

NLB116

■ These motorcycles were old even when this picture was taken aound 50 years ago. *Chron* reader and veteran motorcyclist Ted Cotton recognised the venue as The Bull, Towcester.　　　　NLB117

■ This enormous load was on the move on October 7, 1958, pulled by an ex-military Diamond-T prime mover which dwarfs the Austin A35. According to the scribbled caption on the glass negative, the outfit was called Long John. The Wynn's haulage company is still trading and retired director John Wynn, 73, told us his firm once had 40 of the monster trucks and fitted them with larger cabs. The load was a steel beam being taken from Tipton, Staffordshire, to the nuclear power station at Bradwell, Essex. It weighed 106 tons and was 104 feet long. Six of the girders were taken to Bradwell.　　　　NLB118

■ The stock car racing picture was taken at Brafield Stadium in 1955, says Russ Thomas. He adds: "Team racing was being experimented with using a league system as in speedway. This event was a team race between the Brafield Badgers and the Staines Bulls from Staines Stadium. The 61 car was the captain of the Staines Bulls, Ken Freeman."

NLB119

■ A fun day or gymkhana involving car tyres! Note the Morris Minor convertible and the Triumph Roadster (far right), the car made famous more recently by TV detective Bergerac.

NLB120

■ Older readers will remember the days when what little traffic there was on the roads was very likely made in Britain. That was certainly the case in Regents Square, Northampton, in the 1950s or early 1960s when this picture was taken. A battered Ford "Perpendicular" Popular rounds the corner into Campbell Street, followed by Vauxhall while a more modern Standard waits at the lights. The buildings in the centre still stand but the one on the left has been demolished.

NLB121

■ This Austin Healey 3000 was outside the bottom lodge of the Easton Neston estate near Towcester on a winter's day.

NLB122

■ Mrs P A Nicholls recognised her late father inspecting youngsters' bikes: "I believe the policeman checking the state of the bicycles was my late father, Sgt Jack Symons. He was heavily involved in the Cycling Proficiency Scheme and road safety in general as a member of the traffic department in the Northampton Borough Police. I will always remember that I stepped out from behind a bus in Derngate and was knocked down by a car at this time. When I recovered, I was firmly reminded by my father of advice that he had given to me and which on this occasion I had forgotten. I have been extremely careful ever since! I certainly did not want to cause him any further embarrassment." NLB123

■ The Austin Healey Sprite sliding around a snowy bend was owned and was being driven by *Chronicle & Echo* photographer, the late Alan Burman, probably in the winter of 1963. NLB124

Lambretta LDs are unloaded from Northampton railway sidings before being taken to Norman Stokes's motorcycle shop. Reader David Barry identified the men outside the shop (from left) Mick Berrill, a mechanic with Stokes Motor Cycles, Norman Stokes, who owned the business, Mr Barry himself, who was a mechanic and Matt McGuire, foreman at the firm.   NLB125 & NLB126

LOVE STORY

THIS 50-YEAR-OLD photograph from the *Chron* archives brought memories flooding back for one of the paper's own former staff members.

Patricia Thorpe, whose maiden name was Fiddes, joined the *Chronicle & Echo* as a photographic assistant in 1954 at the age of 21.

Based at the old office on the Market Square, Patricia is pictured here with chief photographer Cyril Arnold, and she thinks the year was about 1956 or 1957.

Patricia said: "I actually trained as a photographer in a commercial studio but I got fed up with it and then I saw an advertisement for a photographic assistant at the *Chron*.

"They had never had a woman in the department before but somehow I got the job.

"People used to send in strange vegetables and misshapen carrots and things and, as far as I can remember, I think this was a two-headed dahlia, which is why we are using a mirror."

Patricia, who is the sister of renowned Northampton artist Chris Fiddes, met her husband Denis at the *Chron*, where he worked as a photographer.

She said: "One of my many tasks in the department was to number, file and organise all the negatives, so I was very interested to hear about the archive.

"My time spent at the *Chronicle* was a happy episode with a lively band of young and talented photographers and reporters."

Denis Thorpe worked at the *Chron* from September 1954 until December 1955. He revealed that he and Patricia had not exactly got off to the best of starts 50 years ago.

"We met by working together in the photographic department, although we didn't think much of each other when we first met," he laughed.

"We only really got together when I was just about to leave. Pat used to do occasional reviews of the Rep for the *Mercury*, and I think she ran out of people to go with because she asked me if I would like to go along.

"We went back to her house to compose the review together and that was it. She used to keep all the photographers in order so we knew our place."

Denis worked in Birmingham and at the *Daily Mail* in Manchester before moving to the *Guardian* where he worked until retiring 10 years ago.

The picture of the two-headed dahlia was also recognised by former *Chron* journalist Ken Nutt, who still lives in Northampton.

"I well remember the two people in the darkroom picture," he said.

"About to take the photograph is Cyril Arnold, who later worked for the noted Northampton portrait photographer Eric Ager."

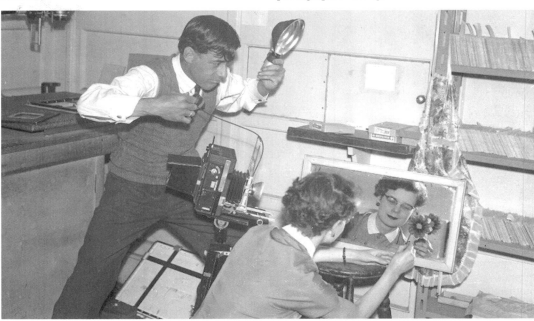

YOUNG 'UNS

Peter Cook says the children in the park were on The Racecourse. "The dark-haired girl at the front is my mother Sheila Cook (née Mckay), now of Hartwell, and the boy standing on the frame on the right of the picture is her brother Pat Mckay, now of Spain.

NLB128

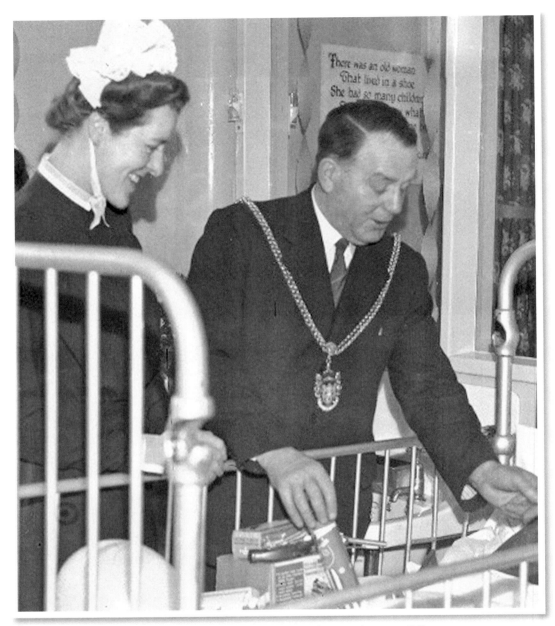

■ Christmas is always a busy time for Northampton mayors and in 1954 it was no different.

Mayor J V Collier OBE is pictured making visits to the General Hospital and the John Greenwood Shipman home where it looks as though he enjoyed playing with the train set. The hospital picture brought memories flooding back for Kathleen Layt, (née Lunn), who was a student nurse in 1958 and who identified the nurse as Sister Elsie Richards and the ward as Nissen Ward. She wrote: "Sister was certainly of the 'old school' and her eyes did not miss a thing. 'Cleaning day' was very important on the ward. Sister made sure every window was open, rain, sun, snow, whatever. The 'outside' workers who cleaned the floors only did so after we, the nurses, had cleaned every surface and even the trolleys were turned upside down and the wheels scraped. My goodness it was hard work but not many germs were left to multiply. A similar procedure took place on the other wards, but I'm sure Nissen Ward was the cleanest."

NLB129

■ Two readers provided information on this picture. Gillian Lock wrote: "This was taken in 1961-62 in Pitsford Village Hall. The event was for the Merry Comrades which my late mother Gladys King (far left) was the leader for Pitsford. I am aged about seven at the front with long hair. Others pictured are Mrs Pryor, Mrs Melay, Jean Wykes, Julia Bartlett, Elaine Williams, Sandra and Lynn Austin, Tim Melay, Joy Shellswell and David Pryor. It was very nice to see this in the *Chron*." And C M Austin added: "My two daughters are in the middle of the front row and the one with white band in second row." The Merry Comrades was a charitable organisation run by the *Chron's* sister paper, the *Northampton Mercury*, and which raised money for good causes.

NLB131

■ The women on the stairs were photographed at J A Perkins in Kings Heath, Northampton, according to Diane Pinson, née Clark, who is at the back on the right. She thinks it was taken as part of a *Chronicle & Echo* competition for office girls in 1968 or 1969. We were also contacted by Mrs D H Flavell, of Bugbrooke, who recognises the woman on the left at the front as her late sister Hazel Frost, later Cumberpatch, who died at the age of 44 in 1985. The family had never seen this photograph of her before.

NLB132

■ This picture brought back memories for Kevin Linnell. He wrote: "I certainly recognise some of the faces. The fair-haired boy on the right I think was called Karl Winters. The boy to his left partially hidden I'm sure is Gary Roach. The lad fifth from the left in the dark top is Darryl Crouch. The boy accepting the trophy could be Robert Hope. They were all in the same year as me at the now-demolished Kings Heath Junior School. I would guess the year would be around 1966-67. Kings Heath School always had a very strong football team so I would guess this was what the trophy was for." NLB133

■ The youngsters waving were outside Northampton High School, "my old school", writes Sandra Warner. The picture shows the front door and the children from the kindergarten (known as "Springhill" and lower school known as "Towerfield") outside the main school in Derngate, Northampton. NLB134

■ These girls are pictured at the Drill Hall, Clare Street, Northampton, and were taking part in a Coronation Queen parade and party, says Di Kennedy. She took part in a similar event. NLB135

■ Co-op Queen Hazel Lack (née Coles) recognised herself in the centre of this group which later rode on a float in Northampton Carnival in the late 1960s. Ms V Steele also recognised some of the girls, many of which worked in the Co-op hairdressers in the Arcade.
NLB136

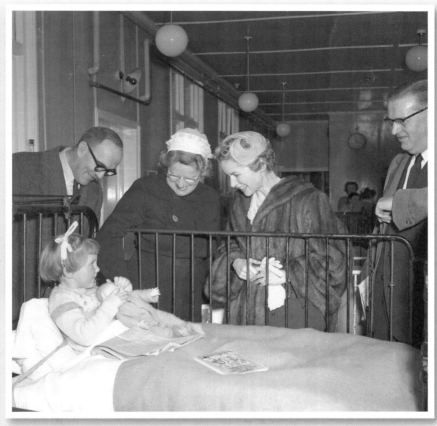

■ This the children's ward at Manfield Hospital, Northampton, in 1958 when Matron Miss E M Edmonds showed around film star Muriel Pavlow, says Ann Church, who was a student nurse at the time. NLB137

■ "My husband is one of the twins in the double pram outside his parents' hot dog stall," writes Mrs J Connell, who somehow got hold of a *Chron* in her Doncaster home! NLB138

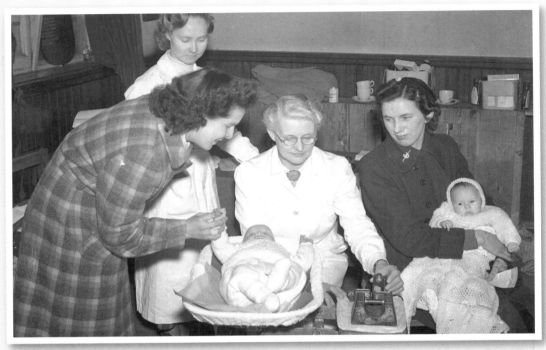

■ The babies at the weigh-in were both identified by *Chron* readers. F Samwell writes: "The picture was taken at Broadmead Baptist Church rooms around Christmas 1953 and it was the welfare baby clinic. The baby on the scales is David Starmer with his mum Hilda. The other baby is Jane, my daughter, with her mother Joan Samwell." Robert Clough adds that the person weighing the babies is his mother Mrs Cora Clough. NLB139

■ Still at the welfare clinic, this picture accompanied an article entitled *Mainly for women*, says Gene of Phippsville. The woman is Miss Barbara Adams, deputy Mayoress at the time, and the child on the left is Timothy, now aged 55. NLB140

■ Six readers supplied information on the retirement of teacher Walter Roberts from St Paul's Junior School, Semilong, Northampton. Alan Webb spotted himself as a pupil, as did Roger Ford, who said Mr Roberts was leaning on his desk. Janet Poole recognised herself along with Christine Jones, Mark Edwards, Martin Parker and Alan Webb. Thanks also to readers D Wright, Mrs V A Baker and Stanley Welsh. NLB141

■ This is the Little Houghton Merry Comrades, run by Mrs Gladys Merritt, says Jennifer Ogden (née Dobson), who is second from the left in the back row. The picture was taken in the mid-1950s at Little Houghton Parish Hall. Margaret Irons also recognised several people. She said: "Two of my daughters, Pat and Susan, are on it. I have the actual picture among all my old photos." The Merry Comrades was a children's club run by the *Northampton Mercury*. NLB142

■ This is the lasting room in the former Northampton College of Technology in St George's Avenue, says Sam Allen, a former part-time student. The man in the white coat on the left was George Lewin, who was in charge.

NLB143

■ Joyce Frost told us: "I had a lovely surprise when I saw the photo of my son Michael receiving an award at the Guildhall. He was about 10 years old at the time. He's 64 now. It was a Church Lads' Brigade (St David's) prize-giving."

NLB144

■ The Roadmender in Lady's Lane, Northampton, a youth club in the 1950s when this picture was taken, is having its ceiling painted, says Brenda Egan (née Pocock), who is second from the left.

NLB145

■ Doris Daly says the double wedding was of her two youngest sisters, Patricia Campion (now Bass) and Cynthia Campion (now Barnes). Barbara Skinner adds: "The couple on the left are Paul Barnes and his bride Cynthia. I remember attending the wedding at St James Church in January 1963. The wedding was a bit late starting as the bride's flowers had not turned up. It snowed hard that day and we followed a snow plough home to Brixworth."

NLB146

■ Miss Painton, a Northampton factory's beauty queen, has been identified by an anonymous reader as Diana Law.

NLB147

■ The choir was from Barry Road School, Northampton, and were pictured around 1953-54, says Diane Garnett, who is in the back row, fourth from the right.

NLB148

■ Sandra Garwood recognised herself placing the poppy cross at Northampton Cenotaph around 1953-55, when she was four or five years old. She was paying tribute to her father's younger brother, Lance Corporal Peter Garwood, who was killed during the Korean War.

NLB149

■ An amazing co-incidence came to light after we published the picture of children playing with toys. Lynda Field explained: "My parents, who live in Kingsthorpe, recognised me. I am the little girl in the centre of the picture in white. My name then was Lynda Goronwy and I was 2-3 years old. I was born in 1952 so I guess the picture was taken 1954-55. We were at what was then called the Community Centre at Thornton's Park, Kingsthorpe, and our mothers were having a sewing lesson. Curiously my picture was also in the *Chron* two days later in a feature I wrote for the Press Association called *Make your own traditions*. My name is now Lynda Field and I write self-help books for Random House. My parents were so delighted with both of the pieces that featured me. The pictures gave them so much pleasure, especially as they were unexpected, so thanks very much."

NLB150

HOW WE MADE
THE *CHRONICLE & ECHO*

OLDER MEMBERS of the *Chronicle & Echo's* staff were delighted when this set of pictures came to light from the depths of our dusty archives!

The sequence shows the production processes of the paper and its weekly sister, the *Mercury & Herald*.

They show (right) Herbie Old operating a Linotype machine. He is re-typing a reporter's story and the machine is setting it in type using a molten lead alloy.

In the days of hand-setting, before Linotypes, the moulds for small letters and capital letters used to be kept in cases on different levels, hence the terms upper case and lower case which we still use in today's computer age.

The stories and pictures are made up into a page and an impression is taken from it with a papier-mâché sheet called a flong.

This is Reg Downes holding it (below).

NLB151 & NLB152

Reg and Pat Shepherd are pictured in the foundry producing a printing plate from the flong (below).

We cannot read the date on the printing plate (right) but the lead story, or splash, is about a road tragedy. The main headline, which we called a screamer, says "Five die, 55 hurt in bus crash". A sub-head adds: "Servicemen's coach cut in half as it hits tree".

Finally, an unknown worker retrieves *Mercury & Heralds* from the press (far right). The main headline reads: "Northants cricket is under threat".

Other pictures we found in decaying cardboard

NLB153

boxes include composing room employees (below), and, on the next page, the newsroom and the *Chron's* Market Square offices in 1959, about the time these pictures were taken.

The Market Square premises were demolished to make way for the Grosvenor Centre expansion shortly after we moved to Upper Mounts in 1978. NLB154, NLB155 & NLB156

NLB157

NLB158

IN THE NEWS

■ "The lady is my grandmother (Granny May) and her husband Reco," writes Jane Burn. "I believe that the photo may have been taken in the 1940s, when they were appearing at the New Theatre in Abington Street, Northampton, as 'Reco and May', a comedy high and low wire act. May was born Mary May Leatherland at Tiffield and later moved with her family to Pastures Farm, Hollowell. She went to school locally and eventually married Herbert Wroe (Reco). May had three children, including my father, Bill Leatherland, who farms at Sheltons Farm, East Haddon. My two aunts, Lucy and Alva, both enjoyed careers in showbusiness in various parts of the world and live in Denmark and Germany. Reco and May toured the country for many years as Circus Reco and featured in a book called British Circus Life by Lady Eleanor Smith. They are both buried in Hollowell churchyard (Granny May died in 1977, aged 65) and are survived by three children, five grandchildren, 12 great-grandchildren and two greatgreat-grandchildren. As for the hat... well Reco was rarely seen without it!"

NLB159

■ Many readers wrote to identify the three people on the election trail in the 1960s. Marion Scott says: "It is Dame Jill Knight, with her husband Monty holding open the car door. On the right is Don Wilson who was to become Mayor of Northampton in 1965. I have spoken to Don who said he helped Dame Jill with quite a few campaigns. Don was 94 a short time ago. He is still alert and active having been organist at Boughton church for many years and he still plays occasionally. He sings in the combined Boughton and Pitsford church choir with us each week and is well loved by everyone."

NLB160

■ This Looking Back picture sparked a flurry of letters from readers who recognised the man as George Markie who worked at the Electric Light Company and whose hobby was carving birds and animals in wood. Among those who wrote to identify the picture were his niece Barbara Grafaske, of Northampton and also Alan Roberts, of Roade, Frank Jeffs, of Northampton and Mr R Shipley, of Northampton.

NLB161

■ This is Northampton Mayor J B Corrin visiting Northampton General Hospital at Christmas, 1964. Jose Corrin writes: "On entering this particular ward, my husband was greeted by Geisha girls. The sister and nurses dressed up and the ward was decorated. A great deal of effort had been made and was greatly appreciated by all. I unfortunately missed this visit as I was ill but he returned from these visits and cooked the Christmas dinner for the whole family."

NLB162

■ Geoff Leatherland wrote with information on the Weedon Fete picture featuring F J C Leatherland's lorry. He said: "F J C Leatherland is a building firm established in Weedon just after the Second World War. The founder of the firm, Fred Leatherland (my father) built his reputation on high-quality individual houses and never needed to advertise in order to attract new business. When he retired about 20 years ago, my brother, John Leatherland, took over, and the firm is still thriving. In his retirement, my dad has restored eight old classic English cars, built 13 Sunbeam S7 and S8 motor bikes from spare parts bought at motor jumble sales, built three steam engines (the largest of which is two metres long) and a couple of steam trains. When John retires from the building firm, his sons, Richard and Andrew will take over the reins. The picture would have been taken in the late 1950s and my brother John is the middle one of the three boys standing up at the front of the lorry. The boy next to him, nearer the camera, is Barry Turner who also still lives in Weedon. The boy furthest away from the camera, sitting down, is Johnny Walker, who also still lives in Weedon. The boy in the Scout uniform at the back of the lorry is Malcolm Ogle who now lives in Daventry." NLB163

■ This picture sparked memories for Keith Gould and Jim Miles who both give the same name for the man in the picture. Mr Miles tells us: "The photograph is of Chief Radio Supervisor "Bagsy" Baker of the Royal Naval Reserve tuning in a B40 receiver in the RNR Receiving Room in Sheep Street. Mr Gould added: "He was in charge of the Royal Naval Reserve office in Sheep Street, where the photograph was taken, probably in the late 1960s or early 70s. The RNR office was situated on the top floor above what was then the National Deposit Friendly Society. Alan Richardson said the equipment was a Superhet naval receiver. The photo was taken in the 1960s when the two men worked together. NLB164

■ Ivor Wilde confirmed that the person addressing the meeting was his father, also called Ivor. He writes: "To the left is my mother Violet. Mother, now aged 85, is still going strong but dad died nearly 21 years ago. I suspect you will have more photos of the election campaigns from the early 1960s, some of which may include my sister Esmé and brother Richard. I recall two other important members from the team at the time, Gordon Roberts and Roger Martin. Electioneering proved to be a great strain and my parents separated in 1965. He married again a few years later and had three more children: Silas, who is now MD of the Wilde Group (based at Harlestone Firs), Seth who is an IT training consultant in London and Felicity who is an interior designer in New York. My sister has just retired from teaching and Richard is a Methodist minister who spent some years in Zimbabwe as a missionary."   NLB165

■ "The lady in your photo was Miss Mabel Gladys Weston who lived in Station Road, Little Houghton," wrote Richard Deacon. "She taught for many years at Brafield School, retiring sometime in the 1960s. The photo was taken in her garden, probably on the occasion of her retirement. I grew up in Little Houghton and remember her as a kindly lady." Reader Gwyneth Grey-Jones confirmed this and added that Miss Weston played the organ at her wedding. Mrs Grey-Jones also went on to teach at Brafield. NLB166

■ The kart driver on the Wall of Death is Roy Cripsey and was pictured performing at Butlins at Skegness, says Dee O'Neill, who went to school in Skegness with his daughter Jane.

NLB167

■ Several readers told us the couple were Colonel Stockdale and the Hon Mrs Stockdale of Mears Ashby Hall, Mears Ashby.   NLB168

■ This picture was identified by Mrs R Pearcey, of West Haddon, who said it was of the Rev T Long. She writes: "He is looking at a piece of wood out of the church roof which the death watch beetle had eaten."   NLB169

■ The wedding couple are Kathleen Jordan and Trevor Stapleton who were married at Mount Pleasant Baptist Church, Northampton. The bride's cousin, David Jordan, of Kingsthorpe, told us the groom's father Fred Stapleton was the borough treasurer at the time. He couldn't remember the date, but a former neighbour of the couple, Sylvia Burn, of Debdale Road, Northampton, got in touch to tell is it was March 27, 1954. Thanks also to Iris Wright and Christine Forskitt who emailed to say the couple now live in Shepperton. NLB170

■ The lady with the dogs was Nina Hill, who lived at Pear Trees, Station Road, West Haddon, says Kathie Shepperson. She was known all over the country for her breeding and showing of daschunds and won many prizes. NLB171

■ Tony Cooper identified the bus tour party as a group from Northampton who went to America. Mr Cooper is on the picture and he thinks the tour it was organised by the *Chron*. They visited New York and Washington and Northampton, Massachussetts. He recognises the man second from the left as Richard Field, a *Chron* journalist, and the woman in the hat was a local headteacher Mary Milburn. NLB172

■ Mr C Osbourne and George Twiselton both agreed that it this taken in The Humphrey Rooms, meeting place and headquarters of Northamptonshire Natural History Society and Field Club, on March 16, 1964. The occasion was the second Humphrey Lecture and pictured are, left to right, Mr G Pretlove, lecturer Dr David Dewhirst, and Mr R D Glenn. The lecture was entitled *"The Dust in Space"*. NLB173

■ The lady is Molly Tolliday, said Gordon Currey. He writes: "She, along with her husband Albert, kept the Red Earl public house on the Spencer estate in the mid-1960s. The handing over of the plate of money was probably in the lounge and a result of a collection for charity that Molly would organise with talent nights and various other functions. Although Albert's name was above the door, it was Molly who ran a great public house with an iron fist. One icy stare from her was enough to make your blood run cold and commanded complete respect from all who went in there. Sadly, several years ago, it fell into decline and was eventually knocked down to make way for housing."

NLB174

■ The group of gentlemen above right were probably snapped at a reunion dinner for the Northampton Nomads Football Club, says Molly Covington. Her late father, Arthur Swan, is fifth from the right. NLB175

■ Two readers recognised TV personality and former London Zoo supervisor George Cansdale. Tony Ward remembered he appeared a lot on children's television in the 1950s and Dave Reed recalled he had his own show called *All About Animals* and guested on *Blue Peter*.

NLB176

■ Hazel Morrison writes: "The man front left is my father, Faulkner Gammage, of Duston. He was the Northampton Coroner for many years and also a local solicitor. I just can't remember the lady next to him, although she is very familiar. Then it's my mother, Margo Gammage, who is 92 and still living in our home in Duston, then Edith Mary and Peter Wilson (he was also a solicitor in Kettering). I would imagine the photo was taken early to mid-1960s, maybe at a legal dinner and possibly at the old Salon at Franklin's Gardens, or maybe Wicksteed. It was lovely to see the photo of my Dad again (he died in 1970). The years disappeared and, for a moment, it could have been yesterday."

NLB177

■ The bride was Miss Diana Deterding, eldest daughter of Mr and Mrs Henry Deterding, of Newnham Grounds, says Avril Maycock. NLB178

■ The sculptor is Leslie Higgins, who lived in Hardingstone and worked for Mettoy, says an anonymous reader. NLB179

■ Miss Battle of Britain is Beryl Goodridge, who won the title around 1954, says Mrs S A Watson, who used to work with Beryl in the Northampton borough treasurer's department. Beryl married Guernsey man Gordon Simon in 1954 and moved to the Channel Islands.

NLB180

■ Lots of readers responded to the choir picture and between them have named most of the ladies! The choir was from Long Buckby WI and had just won a silver cup. The conductor was Nell Frost, who was married to a *Chron* typesetting room overseer, which might account for the publicity! Gwennie Wilkes recognised herself and her sister on the picture and says she is still an active member of the village WI, although her sister has died. The pianist was Fred Bandey, Mrs Frost's brother. Rosemary Leonard spotted her mother, Nellie Walduck, and Barbara Fuller also recognised her mother, Gertie Kennell. Thanks also to EG Johnson and Michael Rauh, who also supplied information.

NLB181

■ The lecturer in this picture is Eric Chapman, area Civil Defence officer for west and south of Northamptonshire and he is talking to members of the Women's Voluntary Service in about 1963, says Joyce Herbert. She recalls that Mr Chapman lived at Nether Heyford and was a former sergeant in the Metropolitan Police. He attended the Harrow train crash disaster in 1952.

NLB182

■ David Smith recognised his father George in this picture of a presentation at Northampton shoe factory Crockett and Jones. He was for many years secretary of the firm's sports and social club. Former assistant factory manager Keith Anderson thinks this could be a presentation of the Crockett Cup and recognises Mr and Mrs Percy Jones, John Eyton-Jones and George Dazeley. The Crockett Cup for bowls is still being competed for.

NLB183

■ The portrait being unveiled is that of Alderman H A Glenn, chairman of the board of Northampton Town and County Building Society, which eventually became Nationwide, says Peter Forrester. Alderman Glenn is seated with his wife. This information comes from Alderman Glenn's granddaughter, adds Mr Forrester.

NLB184

■ Philip Chown was delighted to see a picture of his father Alderman Cyril Chown (centre) with Earl Spencer, grandfather of the present earl (left) and Harold Peach. George Twiselton and an anonymous reader confirmed this information.   NLB185

■ The tramps belong to Northamptonshire Aero Club which always held a Tramps Ball in November, says Edna Islip. She thinks the picture was taken around 1949 and recognises secretary of the club, William "Sunshine" Parry.   NLB186

■ This dates from the mid-1950s and was taken to mark the formation of the Northampton branch of the British Alsatian Association, says Robert Coles. The gentleman sitting on the table is Don Ruthwell, next to him is Mr Coles's grandfather Norman Sanders with his dog Captain and next is Mr Matheson and his large black Alsatian Thunder. He was unable to identify the fourth person but George Rowland writes: "I am the person you could not identify! Yes, I'm still here at 91 years. How's that? I started the Northants Dog Training Club and was also a member of the Northants British Alsatian Association when it started. My dog Otto was obedience champion at Crufts." Robert Rowland recognised his father and added that he was obedience championship judge at Crufts in the mid-1970s.

NLB187